Royal Chi Meditation

Uzoma Nwosu, M.D.

Work has to be carefully balanced with rest and meditation.

(Earthing Medicine]

Earth Breathing

Earth Energy

Manufactured in the United States.

Library of Congress catalogue in-publication data. Nwosu, Uzoma Chika Nnadozie

Author: Uzoma Nwosu, M.D.

Edited by Charisma

Key Words: 1. Chi 2. Love 3. Peace 4. Energy 5. Power 6. Breath 7. Movement 8. Gold

This book is not intended to be used as a
substitute for medical advice and treatment.

Always look up words you do not understand in
a Standard English dictionary.

Table of Contents

Preface

The purpose of this book is to give you a tool to experience a meditation system from Africa, the continent known as the origin of our species.

Modern humans, Homo sapiens, are thought to have evolved in Africa 50, 000 to 100,000 years ago before migrating outside the continent into Asia and Europe. One key differentiating feature between modern humans and their bi-pedal ancestors is the development of a bigger brain in a process called Encephalization. One of the key observations in evolution is the development of newer and better methods of living as manifested by the use and sophistication of tools. Developing these new methods is thought to have happened gradually but a greater advancement towards modern behavior is believed to have happened 40, 000-50,000 years ago. Some of these changes include the specialization of tools, use of animal skin as clothing, burial of the dead, organization of personal space, use of jewelry, visual arts as in cave drawings, and the development of rituals.

These advancements towards modern human behavior are thought to be related to an expansion of human consciousness. While some scientists believe that this expansion had been gradual, others suggest that there was a revolutionary expansion that happened and which coincided with the development of more modern behavior. Consciousness which is being awake, self aware and able to make voluntary movement(s) is thought to have developed in lower life forms as an energy saving feature that allows for better maneuverability in the physical universe. In humans, it is thought that special changes in the anatomy, physiology and biochemistry of the brain occurred to enhance the use of this energy saving mechanism.

Meditation can be considered a practice that allows for a better access to this 'consciousness' which has been described as 'high consciousness' and is apparently not run by conventional human energy.

Meditation is associated with a more stable central nervous system that is more emotionally stable and that is less prone to human to human violence which may be driven by anger. Development of a more robust central nervous system probably allowed more community harmony which led to efficiencies that helped advance communities and allowed for more leisure time that led to more abstract thinking which is manifested in visual arts, dance, healing and other forms of artistic and scientific expression.

With advancements in language that co-developed with the mind, humans had the necessary spatiotemporal co-ordination provided by higher consciousness that is necessary to hunt down huge prey such as the Elephant. The ability to bring down big prey is associated with development of modern human behavior such as burying of the dead.

Meditation is known to be associated with improved cognition and an enhanced ability to solve every day problems that can lead to life satisfaction which can be considered the basis of happiness.

Consider this book, a brief, but yet potent artistic way to introduce you to one the most important meditation systems developed by the ancient Africans at a time period that should be dated because of its global significance.

The Igbo

Igbo is one of the three major tribes of Nigeria and produced Dr. Nnamdi Azikiwe and General Aguiyi-Ironsi, the first two Nigerian leaders. Chinua Achebe, Phillip Emeagwali, Chimanda Adichie, Bennet Omalu, and a host of others are Igbo.

Igbos suffered a disastrous setback following the failed secessionist state of Biafra. However, it is widely believed that the Igbos will make a comeback given the tenacity of the Igbo spirit. The tenacity is embedded in the language and culture of the Igbo.

The Igbos believe that every individual has a Chi that determines the destiny of that individual. In addition, they believe in God (Chi-ukwu) who is the Big Chi and the overall determinant of destiny. If an individual falls off a palm tree; it is the Chi.

Igbo has a hierarchical structure that ranges from a lower Nze to the higher Ọzọ priest, which leads eventually to the King known as the Eze. Rising in rank depends on meditation and expansion of consciousness which is marked by the ability to positively express the Chi. Ascension is marked by ability to display loving kindness and philanthropy, and the absence of violence.

The earth is considered an authority in Igbo - a deity. That means the earth has the capacity to punish or bless. 'Anagọlụ' is a word that has the root word for bless 'gọ' which suggests 'blessed by the Earth.' In fact, a common word for Igbo culture itself is Omenana which suggests 'Happening on Earth' or 'Earth Happenings.' Igbo life revolves around the Earth and a favorable relationship with the earth is a necessity for a good and pleasant life.

The knowledge that the earth is a source of healing and wellness is not unique to Igbo. Yoga and Tai Chi are similar culturally based healing and relaxation techniques that acknowledge the healing qualities of the earth.

The Chi

The ancient Africans believe humans have a spirit called mmụọ, a soul known as mụ, and a 'body' known as 'arụ' or a 'soul body' known as 'arụ mụ.' The soul is naturally peaceful and loving and in its top form.

In addition, every person has an internal Chi, which is their personal energy that determines their destiny. The Chi is like the soul-peaceful and loving. However, because the Chi is the interface between the soul and the body, the inside and outside worlds, it is vulnerable to being 'corrupted'.

The life of a person is directed from the internal Chi to the outside world and physical universe.

All human experiences occur in the Chi.

Experience is only possible in the Chi. Without the Chi, you will have no experience. The Chi is the internal energy of an individual that is converted and translated in the physical world.

The feelings and emotions that compel a person to neglect his parents or love his child are in the Chi. If a man shows you compassion, it is the compassionate energy in the Chi that is translated into acts of kindness.

Care or lack of care is the translation of the energy directed from the Chi.

For example, my ability to bring this message to you first occurred in my Chi, and its expression into the physical universe is directed from the Chi.

When you listen to music, yes there is a speaker out there blasting the sound, but the sound can only be heard within, by the Chi. All our experiences are within. Even sexual pleasure can only by experienced within. The penis and the vagina are useless in the absence of the Chi.

Likewise, all our experiences in the physical universe are from and are experienced from the Chi.

The Chi or consciousness energy is more important than your job. You see, you may manifest a job, business or friends and then someone could cause you to lose them but I don't think you should worry. The most important thing is that you still have your Chi and that it is intact and in a good condition. So long as you have your Chi, you can manifest a better job, business, or even friends in a different environment.

CHIDUME

Chi is energetic

Chapter 1-   Royal Meditation

Royalty is an exceptional human being with responsibility and optimum love for self, family, community, land, animals, earth and celestial objects.

Meditation is an irreplaceable tool that gives the Royalty access to the Higher human powers and consciousness that enables him/her avoid jealousy, wickedness, meanness, fear, apathy, sadness, etc and other uncomfortable emotions that will invariably have a negative impact to the health and wellbeing of a community.

One of the challenges of the modern human is to develop the capacity to experience their choice. For example, one may prefer to listen to the sound of nature at night rather than living next to the highway or railway and being continuously disturbed by noisy traffic. Meditation gives one access to higher consciousness and the Chi, so that we can begin an endless journey of manifesting our choosing, that is being cause, rather than being the effect of the universe.

Man is unique because of our ability to work together on common goals. For example, humans have the power of hundreds of thousands of individuals. Unlike, the wildebeest in the Serengeti that also number hundreds of thousands; humans are able to deploy tools such as innovation and technology that have enormous impact on geography and terrain.

The ability of the human race to mount an effective response depends on effective communication between hundreds and thousands of Chis communicating and co-ordinating their experiences and actions.

So one of the responsibilities of the Royal is to provide a platform for communication, based on meditation that leads to more effective communication between him and his people.

Technique of Royal Igbo Meditation

Earthing

Similar to Yoga, Tai Chi and other meditation practices you need to select a quiet and safe area in your home or neighborhood. Although an individual has great latitude with time selection, it may be important to rhyme meditation with the beginning or end of the day or other relevant events such as the beginning of a performance.

It is important to select an area where one has direct contact with the earth, such as the ground floor or basement level of a house, or in a garden. A mat can be placed on the earth for comfort and protection from insects and other undesirable objects and living things. Of course, this requirement should not prevent someone on the 100th floor of a New York apartment building from participating in meditation.

After feeling the feet on the earth and recognizing the earth as an authority, the next step is to sit on the earth in what is known as 'i tu kwu ana.' This is the very famous cross-legged position known in Yoga and similar cultural practices as the Lotus position. This reconciling a person with the earth can be described as 'Earthing.'

Lotus position-Eugenio Hansen

The Lotus position is a way to achieve 'oneness' or 'unity' with the earth. This association with the earth is important. To give you a clearer picture of this position, I would like to introduce you to the word for waist which is 'ukwu.' Ukwu contains the verb 'kwu' which is 'speak.' The waist is used in non-verbal 'speaking' or communication. It is the anatomical structure used to contact and communicate with the earth. It has relevance in sitting and lying on the earth while meditating. Etymologically speaking, 'I tu kwu ana' means to 'speak as one with the earth.'

Silence

The intent of meditation is to connect an individual to loving and peaceful universal energy from which we are made. We do this by connecting to the universal energy in the earth through the waist.

 After making contact with the earth, the next activity is silence. Silence is known as Igba Chi nkịtị (silence the Chi) or Igba ụwa nkịtị (Silence the world).

We need to silence our personal energy (the Chi), because it is affected by the negative energy accumulated by encountering other humans and other life challenges.

In this period of silence, we are communicating with the peaceful soul, the universal energy, the earth energy which is a loving peaceful energy. This energy does not necessarily speak a human language as in vocal words but humans can translate this communication into human words and action. Typically, the communication is about positive emotions or energy such as love, peace and joy. This energy of peace, love and joy can be translated into thoughts, words and action of peace, love and joy. A peaceful Chi (personal energy) is known as 'Udochi.' Evidence of meditation, is seen in the community as acts of kindness and philanthropy.

Expressing the loving energy of the earth is embodied in the principle of Anagekwu (the earth will speak) which allows an individual to contact and communicate peaceful and loving information from the earth.

Human representatives of the earth who may be high ranking officials of a town have to create peace and harmony in the society. So in order to give sound judgment, these individuals need to know meditation extensively.

The Heart

Obi, the word for heart, contains the verb 'bi' which is 'to live.' Life is not possible without a beating heart. A close variant, Obi, is the word for a man's central house, where the life of the household is based. After lying down, the next step is to apply the heart to the earth, the same way a mother applies the heart of her baby next to her heart. This is called 'Obi iru ana' or 'heart reaching the earth.' This is an important way to relax the heart and bring it down to earth, so that it knows less palpitation or worry. Some find lying on the Left or heart side of the body very relaxing because they can put their heart close to our mother earth.

Obi, the word for a family central house is phonologically similar to the word for heart 'Obi'. Family activity is directed from the Obi.

Breathing technique; Earth Breathing(Umeana)

Umeana is a word that is used to refer to peace and tranquility and contains the word Ume (breath/energy) and Ana (earth). Whenever one consciously breathes while lying on the earth, 'Earth breathing'(umeana) is being practiced. Consciousness is characterized by voluntary action. This relaxed type of breathing that is deep and slow has been studied, scientifically, and is known to be useful in stress, anxiety, depression, post traumatic stress disorder, anger, frustration and similar negative emotions

(Brown and Gerbarg, 2012). In addition, it is known to lower blood pressure. This type of breathing is known to upgrade the parasympathetic nervous system which is the relaxing branch of the Central Nervous System. Breathing can be paced at about 5 breaths per minute, and only about 20 minutes of practice is required daily although some recommend up to 1 hour of daily practice.

Proposed mechanism of lowering blood pressure	
Decreased Cortisol	Cortisol is a key marker of the body's stress response system. Meditation is associated with decreased blood Cortisol levels. Cortisol is a steroid hormone that causes salt and water retention which can cause an increase in blood pressure.
Increased Nitrogen Oxide (NO) production	Meditation is associated with increased NO production. NO is a smooth muscle relaxant and causes a decrease in blood pressure. Viagra (sildenafil) and Arginine cause a net increase in NO.
Decreased Sympathetic nervous system activity and Increase in parasympathetic nervous system activity.	Adrenaline and Nor-adrenaline which are products of the sympathetic nervous system are blood vessel constrictors and can cause high blood pressure.

To ensure that the diaphragm is being used, one can gently place the palm over the abdomen and observe it rise with inspiration and go down with expiration.

The nose is typically used in Earth breathing and is known as 'imi.' 'Imi' contains the verb 'mi' which is 'deepen.' The nose speeds up the velocity of the air traveling to the lungs and makes it possible for the air to reach the lungs without excessive energy expenditure. This increase in velocity is known as the Venturi effect in Physics. While breathing out, an expiratory grunt can also be made which is known as 'Ude' and is a known yoga breathing technique. 'Udemezue' (My Ude/wellbeing is complete) is an expression one makes when things are going their way and suggests that this type of breathing helps in achievement.

Most of the energy production in the human body is made in the cell mitochondria which is the 'power house' of the cell. Here, oxygen is split and combined with hydrogen ions produced in the Krebs or Citric acid cycle to make water. The electron gradient created by this reaction is used to create ATP (Adenosine Triphosphate) which is the energy currency of the cell. Energy production in the human body is oxygen dependent and shuts down in the absence of oxygen. It takes about 3 minutes to die in the absence of oxygen, and this explains why, in the wild, predators seize the neck of animals to prevent them from breathing.

At the Mara River of the Serengeti, a common move by the Crocodile is to drag prey underwater so it drowns.

The Krebs or Citric acid cycle yields a negligible amount of energy compared to the Oxygen dependent Oxidative-phosphorylation that occurs in the mitochondria.

Understanding this helps us avoid energy rich foods such as simple sugars, flour and other processed foods that contribute to the Obesity epidemic. Obesity is a major cause of Hypertension,

Diabetes Mellitus, Cancer, Heart Disease and a host of other diseases.

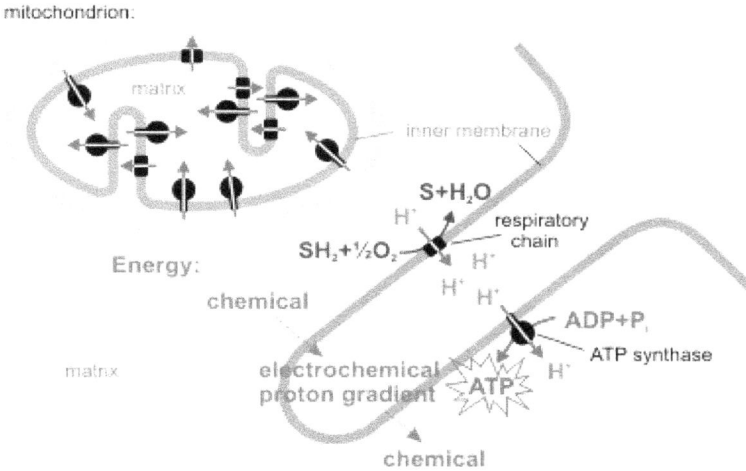

mitochondrion:

matrix

inner membrane

S+H_2O

SH_2+½O_2

H⁺

respiratory chain

H⁺

H⁺ H⁺

ADP+P

ATP synthase

Energy:

chemical

matrix

electrochemical proton gradient

ATP

H⁺

chemical

Oxidative phosphorylation in the mitochondria showing that the production of ATP in the electron transport chain is coupled with the conversion of Oxygen into water. ATP is the energy currency of the body. Image by Darekk2.

We have already noted that meditation energizes and calms a person. Now, we have also noted that oxygen in the breath is the source of practically all human energy. This is why in Igbo the word for breath and energy are the same-'ume.' Ume contains the verb 'me' which is 'to do' or 'make' because your energy is what you use to create your life. We have also already noted that higher consciousness evolved as an energy saving mechanism that accords, among other things, better spatial orientation and the ability to maneuver the planet, so we can readily understand that meditation is an energy saving process.

In Igbo, the word for meditation can be considered as 'izu ike' which is commonly understood as 'rest' but means to 'merge energy or power.' 'Izu' is combining, pool, put together, or merge while 'ike' is energy, power or strength.

Izu ike (Resting, meditating, merging energy/power/strength). A lion resting on the Earth. The word for lion, Ọdụm, also means 'My Advisor.' Image-Kevin Pluck

My experience is that merging the emotional energy from the breath and the physical energy from food and physical activity requires patience, experimenting and individual variations. A wise individual creates a balance that gives them the emotional condition that is satisfying and the one that leads to happiness.

While meditating and keeping silent, recurrent thoughts begin to subside as one gets more in contact with the higher consciousness. These recurrent thoughts are often negative and are energy depleting.

Contacting the higher consciousness is being with the Chi energy and from which we create a gentle, loving, peaceful and joyful life.

The body as two in one

As mentioned earlier, consciousness was thought to have developed in lower life forms as a means of better assessing themselves and their spatial relationship in the physical planet. The more conscious a person is, the more capable they are in the physical planet. The human body actually has two halves, a right and left half and co-ordination between the two halves is necessary for optimal operation. This 'two in one' nature is acknowledged by passing the breath from the earth to the head on either side of the body, and vice versa.

The word 'Umeana' has two meanings; Earth energy and Earth breathing. This type of breathing makes a person contact the 'energy saving' higher consciousness that is provided for humans on earth by mother earth, and allows the body to retain more energy to perform physiological functions such as body repair. Breathing relaxation is known to improve health outcomes even in patients with heart disease.

Chapter 2- Hope and Faith

The heart is one of the most powerful organs in the body and guarding the heart is a necessity. One part of the body (other than the head) no one wants to be shot at is the heart. Heart disease is a major killer that prevents people from reaching their desired goals on this planet. Once the heart begins to dysfunction, other organs such as the brain are affected, starting a downward spiral that cannot be readily reversed. Major assignments are not to be given to someone with a dysfunctional heart or the faint hearted.

In Igbo, when it comes to accomplishments, the heart is the physical organ that is involved in the forefront. This is why the Igbo say 'Obi idi na ife'- that is that your 'heart has to be in it.' If ones heart is not in something, very little is usually accomplished. Many of the effective human beings we know who became famous politicians, scientists or artists have their hearts deeply embedded in their tasks. A man cannot say he truly loves a woman when his heart is not embedded in the woman. The Hollywood phrase 'heart throb' says it all, because love and interest is a hearty phenomenon.

The Chi, the internal spiritual energy of a person, works closely with the heart in goal accomplishment. This phenomenon is captured in the phrase 'Chimobi'-Chi knows the heart. The Heart and the Chi work in tandem to bring the desires of a person known as the Nchọ into existence.

Encouragement is known as 'nkasị obi' which contains the words/verbs nka (aging), sị (stop) and obi (heart). To encourage someone is to 'strengthen their heart' or to ask them to have a youthful heart that can be accessed through meditation.

Faith

According to the Merriam-Webster dictionary, faith is a strong belief in someone or something. Others have described faith as 'hope in what we cannot see', while Hebrew 11 verse 1 describes faith as '..substance of things hoped for and evidence of things not seen.' Biblical sources suggest that hope and faith are closely related.

While the translation of Igbo to English should not be regarded as straight forward, 'ntụkwasị obi ' is generally accepted to refer to 'faith.' A superficial way to look at 'ntụkwasị obi' (faith) is to translate it as 'place the heart.' This suggests that to have faith in something is to 'place the heart' in it. However, the word 'ntụkwasị' contains three verbs 'ntụ' (throw) , kwa (push) and 'sị' (stop). In reality if you place something somewhere, you have moved(throw/push) and then 'stopped' or 'stilled 'it. So a deeper way to understand 'ntụkwasị obi' (faith) is 'stilling the heart' or 'storing the heart.' When a person has faith in something, one does not have any worries about it. The heart has been 'chilled' calmed and is not shaking, trembling or having palpitations.

Generally speaking, anything that can calm the heart, including singing, earth breathing and physical exercise are faith instruments. These activities give someone general faith in life. Earth breathing/Meditation has been studied scientifically and has been shown to slow the heart and strengthen heart function. This, more or less, suggests that Earth breathing (umeana) is a way to 'still the heart' and have faith.

Stones and the heart

Although, earth breathing may be sufficient to develop faith, there are a few add on activities or practices that may be useful in instilling faith.

Crystals are a wide range of semi-precious stones that are used in a wide range of healing activity. They are generally not accepted by main stream medicine, but many practitioners swear to their efficacy.

While this book is not about stones or crystals; Rose quartz, clear quarts and Agate deserve some attention. These stones are recommended to be placed on the central chest or heart chakra, and have been observed to calm the 'heart' and emotions, and can be considered faith instruments. Placing these stones on the central chest, heart chakra, can be performed in tandem with 'Earth breathing' for the removal of ajịja (stress) and other negative emotions.

Obi is the word for heart and Chest. Heart proper is known as 'Nkpụlụ obi.' The heart is closely related to the Chi and is recorded in the phrase Chimobi (Chi knows the heart). The heart is also related to the soul or mind. 'Kedụ ife ibu no obi?' is 'what are you carrying in your heart/chest?' or 'what do you have in mind?'
Stones can be carried on the chest to achieve certain objectives.

Those who undertake challenging tasks that require plenty of faith, may consider placing larger pieces of rock known as 'Mkpume' over the chest, to 'still the heart' or turn the heart into 'stone.' Selecting stones, rocks and crystals, should be reserved for individuals more knowledgeable about this area of expertise.

These stones are used to strengthen the heart and emotions so that your heart is strong (Obisike). Someone with a strong heart is described as 'onye obi ya bụ mkpume' or 'a person who's heart is stone.'

'Onye ji azụ eku ume' is a person who breathes with the back and is associated with deep abdominal breaths that are energizing and relaxing and is a major part of Earth breathing. This type of breathing is associated with strong will and is known to strengthen the 'heart.' Although often used in a negative manner, a strong willed person is known as 'onye obi ya di na azụ'- a person who's heart is at the back. This type of strong will may be necessary in times of stress or in times when an individual needs to manifest something important for themselves and/or their family.

The relationship between the back, the heart and the emotions explains why cupping is often done at the back to strengthen a person. Cupping is good for removing stress (ajịja). The use of stones/crystals before, during, and after cupping has been described as useful.

Ancient African cupping. Image courtesy of Wellcome Trust.

Modern cupping kit

Hope

Hope is known as Nchekwube which contains the verbs Nche (waiting), kwu (speak) and be (end, stop). Hope is a meditative state characterized by waiting to express an event or an outcome. So someone who has hope has the words they want to express already formed and are just waiting to deliver them at the right time. For example, if you have the hope to be the United States President you may want to start practicing your acceptance speech. If you hope to get married one day, you might want to start looking at wedding gowns and start practicing how you would say your own very special version of "I do."

Kwube (speak and then stop) is an important way of being because communication is a two way activity. An individual speaks then waits for the other person to speak. Most of our problems in communication happen because of our inability to listen. When we speak, it is important that we stop then listen to what the other party is saying to ensure that they got what we are saying in the first place and we got what they were saying, so that if necessary we can both make another effort to deliver the communication.

> **Most of the problems in communication happen because of our inability to listen.**

This ability to listen in communication is priceless. In the Igbo language, the word to marry contains the verb 'nụ' which is listen. This suggests that marriage is 'listening' to one another. This listening starts when a man first spots the woman. There might be some non-verbal communication that a man with an expanded consciousness is designed to listen to. Movement of the hips is well known as non-verbal communication and a talented woman can use her hips to communicate to men that she wants to be loved. The word for waist is 'ukwu' and contains the verb 'kwu' which is to 'speak.'

As mentioned earlier, the waist is a point of contact with the earth in sitting and lying meditation. Its main use is the contact and communication of loving, peaceful and joyful information from the earth to humans. This loving, peaceful and joyful information from the earth to the Chi is the source of human power and is celebrated as Chibụike (Chi is power) or Chijume (Chi holds energy).

The hips can be used in communication.

Again hope is the meditative state characterized by 'deferred communication.' One of the helpful things in the state of hope are the things you already have, the things that are assured, guaranteed or certain. For example, if you are looking for a job as a doctor, one thing you are assured of is that you are already a doctor and you have your certificate to prove it. These assurances are the things known as 'ife e ji n'aka' and are the pillars to the place of hope.

In Africa, Kings held their titles in their hand. These titles are their assurances that they are indeed King. In the modern world, your credit card or cash in your pocket are the assurances that you can pay for what you desire.

One is expected to have hope at all times. There are people who act more like the Hyena than a human and are known to hurt many people. One can stop feeling like their victim by having hope. That is having the words we wish to express when we see them. Strong communication should be readied. " You Hyena……" is an appropriate communication for such people and should be said with 'gusto.' We should keep our eyes open in the community, seeking out the 'Hyenas' so they can receive the communication they deserve with 'gusto.' This preparedness is a mental state that is strengthening and encouraging.

Chapter 3 Physical Activity

The physical body is your tool for the manifesting of the desire of the Chi in this physical world and needs to be in a good or excellent condition. Individuals with great bodies such as Arnold Schwarzenegger, Brad Pitt, Angelina Jolie or Denzel Washington are highly regarded and are paid millions of dollars in Hollywood.

Most people are already very familiar with the health benefits of physical activity and how they can lead to a longer life span and how they can ameliorate common medical conditions such as Hypertension and Diabetes Mellitus.

<u>Diet and nutrition</u>

Physical activity must be accompanied with a healthy diet rich in fiber, fruits, vegetables, nuts, healthy protein, and other nutrients. It is wise to consult a registered nutritionist. Here are a few products from Africa that are traditionally known for their healthy benefits.

Food Product		Benefits
English	**Igbo**	
Yam	Ji	Rich in fiber. Perhaps the best staple. Superior to potatoes and rice. Low glycemic index.
Okra	Okwụlụ	Good source of fiber, may lower blood glucose, low glycemic index, may lower cholesterol, anti-

		oxidants. Plant Viagra
Bitter leaf	Onugbu	Same as Okra
Kola nut	Ọji	Stimulant, contains caffeine. Also contains the active ingredient in chocolate, theobromine
Bitter Kola	Akị inu	Energy, improvement in respiratory function, sexual stimulant, body rejuvenation
African mango	Ọgbọnọ	Weight loss, may lower cholesterol, may lower blood sugar,

Most developed nations have leisure institutions that promote physical activity that can be easily accessed by the community. Some of these institutions offer Dance, Yoga, Tai chi, Chi Kong, Kung fu, Karate, Taekwondo, etc that are known to be good for the body. The martial arts are good for self confidence, especially for those who are fearful that they would be assaulted.

Royal Walking/Earth Walking

Walking is known as 'iga ije' (going on a journey) and is well known for its therapeutic benefits in weight loss, Hypertension, Diabetes, Stress, Anxiety, Depression, and similar conditions.

Walking increases blood flow to the brain and stimulates the release of hormones and other messengers that help in creating a youthful body that can learn and memorize more. Physicians recommend 30 minutes of brisk walking 3 to 4 times a week.

Walking is a good way to visit the places that are good for your health which include gardens, parks or streams where you can relax and meditate, if the weather permits. It is also a way to know the earth (I ma Ana). Someone who knows their community and environs has a head start in solving their problems. Walking and knowing the earth allows an individual to reconcile and associate themselves with the earth while walking. Earth breathing should also be practiced while walking and the principle of two (Ibụa) can be used here. The word for two contains the verb 'bụ' which is 'being.' The body is actually a two in one, in the sense that there is a left side and a right side. A good body has a harmonious relationship between the two sides. It is now known from scientific studies that left handed individuals have a world view that is somewhat different from Right handed individuals.

While walking, it is helpful to alternately practice earth breathing by breathing into say the Left foot up to the back of the head, then breathing down to the earth again. Then breathing in from the Right foot, up into the back of the Right head, then breathing down into the earth. The same can be repeated up the front part of the body alternating to the other side. When appropriate, one can breathe from both legs up either through the front or back of the body, or into the whole body as a person wishes.

This is meditation on the go.

Royal Dance
Royal dance (Egwu Ndi Eze) is a special type of dance practiced for the protection of the spirit or the Chi energy of an individual. The Igbo word for dance (égwu) contains the verb 'gwu' which is used in Ugwu (hill), Ugwu (dignity) and suggests protection.

Dance (égwu) is pronounced in a positive direction but ègwu, the word for fear, is pronounced in the opposite direction. A protected energy or spirit in a good condition should not have any fear.

Dance is a way to gain confidence and conquer fear which is an impulse that makes us feel insecure and incapable.

 Royal dance starts by feeling the feet on the earth which is a form of reconciliation and association with the earth. Music (Igu égwu, dance hunger) is used to enhance and create a hunger for dance. Once one reconciles themselves with the earth (earthing), the next step is to start moving on the earth with a focus on the feet. Then one can start bouncing on the earth in 'quiet excitement' with the arms dangling.

From the feet, the focus is now moved to the ankles, then the knees, the waist, the belly, the shoulders, then the elbows, the wrist, and back up to the neck. With each shift in focus, another of the areas participates in the dance movement. It is a good way to exercise the joints of the body and relax muscles, tendons and ligaments. One can make patterns and shapes with their body as they deem fit. 30 minutes of dancing about 4 times a week may be sufficient to obtain benefits.

Earth breathing with breathing from the feet (earth) to the head, and back to the earth should be practiced while dancing.

Dancing is known to be medically useful as a form of exercise and has been used to ameliorate Hypertension, Diabetes Mellitus, Stress, Anxiety, Depression and similar emotional conditions.

Push ups
These are good for the upper limb and the pectoral muscles. Being able to do 20 push-ups in one sitting is a good target.

Stretching

Stretching the quadriceps, hamstrings and Iliopsoas muscles and tendons is good for back ache. They also give the leg the flexibility necessary for long walks and other leg actions.

Leopard Crawl (Igbe agụ)

Leopards and Lions are known to squat and move in the squatted position while trying to get near their prey. Humans can also perform this type of movement by squatting and then moving. It is very exhausting and should only be attempted by someone in a good physical condition. This type of exercise rapidly gets the heart pounding and is a good type of cardiac exercise.

A hunter should be fit enough to make this type of movement over long distances so they can get near prey under the cover of tall grass.

Body thrusts

This is a motion characterized by lowering the upper body and then making thrusting positions with the upper limbs as if one is planting seeds.

Pounding motions

One of the cycles of life is the preparation of food. Food preparation is more or less a daily activity in Africa. Prior to the advent of electricity and the electric blender, food such as yam had to be pounded. Yam was (is) pounded in a giant mortar and pestle and the pounding is a very important exercise because it requires securing the feet squarely on the earth, balancing the body on the hips, and then making the pounding motions with the upper arms. This activity gets the heart pounding rapidly and is a good cardiac exercise, especially when one has to do this for a sizeable family or if one is cooking for guests, or for an event.

In the absence of mortar and pestle, a person may choose to mimic the stance and motions of 'yam pounding' and is a good form of exercise.

Mortar and Pestle. Image by 100yen.

Squats

Squats are one of the best exercises and are regularly recommended by Physicians, Physical therapists, and personal trainers. It is known to activate the muscles of the upper and lower body and rapidly increases the heart rate and is obviously a good cardiac exercise.

In Africa, squats have special relevance because a person has to squat before a pot of water can be 'loaded' on their head. The same is true for people who have to carry goods for sale to a market place or to other towns. Strong lower limbs are obviously very useful in most human activity.

Squats are also good for the development of the buttock muscles. These muscles apparently give a woman a greater aesthetic appeal. Evolutionary Psychologists believe the rounded hip is a visual signal used to attract males for mating. As mentioned earlier, the waist is an important point of contact with the earth in meditation and is a tool for non-verbal communication. Women with bigger hips may have communicated better than those without and having these bigger but healthy hips and buttocks may have been an evolutionary advantage. The hips should be used to communicate a message of peace, love and joy to a sexual partner as well as in the community.

The hip as a communication tool. Image by Darkmightyaj

If a person can do fifty squats in one stretch, they can have an olileanya (vision) of gold and say the affirmation; "My Chi has made me wealthy." Health will invariably lead to wealth.

Chapter 4   Gold Meditation

One of the aims of meditation is to bring an individual to a native state that is free from negative emotions but full of love, joy and peace. In Igbo, it is done by connecting a person's energy, the Chi, to the Big or Universal Chi, and the loving energy from mother earth. In order to do this, a person has to reconcile himself with the earth and be willing to be a vessel for communication of the gentle earth energy which is known as 'Ume ana'. This is a healing loving energy that is associated with a relaxed body that takes deep abdominal breaths and is energizing and relaxing. This type of breathing is also known as 'umeana' or 'earth breathing.' Individuals with this earth energy are known to be peaceful, loving, kind, compassionate, humble, honest, and patient and they undertake their tasks with a sense of responsibility that is almost super human.

These people are able to channel the earth's energy of compassion and mercy which is noted in the phrase "Chidiebele"- the Chi is merciful.

A person who is merciful is spiritually and materially rich. A person who can cure blindness with their faith is materially rich because they can take a blind eye which is a material structure and enrich it with the ability to see.

One of the benefits of spirituality is to make a person spiritually rich, because that will invariably result in material wealth. This is because a secular word for spirituality is 'thought.' To deepen your spirituality is to expand the breadth and scope of your thought so they can manifest something that is grand. To deepen ones thought requires learning and experience in the physical world which entails mastery of physical objects. Mastery of physical objects invariably leads to physical objects that have value to humans in the physical world. These are the products and services that can be exchanged with other humans for a reward.

This is why spiritual organizations such as the Vatican bank are worth billions of dollars. Successful Pastors such as Billy Graham have mastered thought or spiritual processes and are translating their knowledge into the Physical world for reward and own private jets. Even those of them that are fraudulent have mastered the art of human deception.

Gold is a precious metal that is highly regarded for its durability and esthetic value. To give you an idea as to the worth of gold, Okra, a super food costs about $4.00 a pound in a supermarket while gold is trading over $16,000 per pound in international markets.

To understand how you can turn anything into gold, we are going to first reconcile ourselves with the earth, but his time the golden earth.

Golden Earth (Ana edo)

The high level of consciousness attained during meditation should be utilized at all times. Whenever a person is walking, it is important to feel the feet and recognize that one is on the earth and that the sun is above (if it is day time). 'Anyanwụ' is 'eye of the sun' but also means 'eye for the sun' and keeping an 'eye for the sun' keeps a person oriented in person (child of earth, nwana) place (earth) and time (position of sun).

Golden earth is a specialized area of the earth that is 'golden.' It is clean and well organized. The trees, shrubs and flowers are in their best state and are of high quality. The ground is covered by clean soil, sand and/or stones. This is the area that is selected for meditation in order to manifest 'gold' in your life. This beautiful spot on earth is known as 'anaedo' or 'golden earth' and is usually located inside a person's compound. It is the spot selected for 'gold' meditation. A person who lives in an apartment complex may seek out such spots in local parks and recreational areas. For example, in New York City, Central Park has many spots that may meet this criterion. The golden earth, gives us the environment to have an excellent meditation that gives us a state of being known as Nsọana (respect for the earth). A person with this state, obeys the law of the earth or land and has a clean record. This state also leads to Nsọedo (respect for gold) which can be understood as respect for high standards and quality.

In the Royal meditation position, the legs are crossed and the arms are also crossed. The cross formation or 'X' is a sign of the Chi. The right palm is gently resting on the left leg and the left palm is gently resting on the Right leg. The neck muscles are relaxed and the head is hanging downwards like a baby in his/her mother's womb. The breath is noticed and then breathing becomes conscious.

In this position, as time goes, a person begins to realize that they are sitting on the earth (inọ ana, togetherness with the earth). Then they realize they are being gently carried by the earth, very gently, virtually unnoticeable. As time goes on the muscles begin to relax and pain begins to slide away. The eyes begin to soften as the eyelid muscles begin to relax.

At this stage pain, sorrow and tears begin to recede. Inside, one begins to feel like a hollow cylinder filled with golden energy. Elements of ajịja (stress) begin to disappear and one may begin to see golden images and color combinations and other golden imagery.

Royal position with Royal Igbo stones known as Carnelian Agate.

There's inter individual and intra individual variations in experiences depending on their length of meditation and the severity of a person's mental condition. Stubborn Ajija (stress), may respond to cupping therapy (ichi ochi). Also, essential oils can be used while meditating, and can be dispensed on the palm and then applied on areas such as the central chest, forehead or top of the head, the navel, or the soles of the feet. They can also be dispensed with an electronic diffuser.

Gold and Earth knowledge

'I ma ana' (Earth knowledge) is a phrase used to describe the phenomenon of knowing the country or city you live in. So you have to know persons, places and timing associated with businesses.

A person with considerable earth knowledge invariably becomes an 'Amana' which is a title given to a person in the community that has a sound knowledge of the town or city. This high ranking person functions like a legislator and judge and has the power to settle disputes and impose fines. 'Amana' contains the verb ma (know) and Ana (Earth) and embodies the phenomenon of 'Earth Knowledge.'

An Amana knows where to find raw gold in the city, if there are gold deposits nearby. This raw gold has to be dug up and then transported to a place where it can be processed. Golden meditation gives you the cognitive power and physical energy that is necessary to co-ordinate the affairs of men in the area of manifesting gold. This ability to harmoniously coordinate the affairs of men enabled early humans hunt big game such as elephants. Abundance of meat allowed communities to prosper and eventually led to kingship as we know it today and helps explain why the elephant tusk is a symbol of kingship.

Purification (Extraction)

The next step is to take the raw gold that has limited value and convert it into pure gold in an extraction process that can be described as purification. This purification process is the heart of the gold making operation and application of this process in any earthly activity yields the gold equivalent.

The basic component here is purification or the removal of the unwanted. If you look at a successful pastor like Billy Graham, he creates spaces where thousands of unhappy and dejected people come and get convinced that God loves them. He is removing the impurities of unhappiness and dejection and replacing it with love and hope. His congregants are walking out feeling better and saying "wow." Donald Trump takes an abandoned property and 'purifies' it and all of a sudden 5000 people want to live there. It's only common sense that a person wanting to rent his apartment fast will have to clean and paint the apartment except you want to attract someone who does not mind dirt who will sooner or later stop paying rent. If you look carefully, there are humans in your life who are impurities in the sense they hamper your progress. Those individuals need to be confronted and removed even if they are members of your family.

Golden Chi
The Igbo talk about a Golden Chi which is known as Chiedo. The word 'Edo' means 'gold.' A person with 'Chiedo' has a personal Chi that has 'golden' energy. This person's Chi is so pure that whatever he gets involved in will turn into gold. This is the so called Midas touch. This is a person with a Chi that is insistent on a high degree of purity in whatever he gets involved in. This high degree of purity can also be understood as a high degree of efficiency. If you write a book in 5 years and you sell 10, 000 copies but Chiedo writes an equivalent book in 5 days and sells 10.000 copies, he is demonstrating 'writing gold.'

Vision and Postulates
Manifesting gold starts with a vision of the final product or service. This vision is known as 'Olileanya' and could be 10

pounds of pure gold in your hands. This vision is communicated via a postulate known as 'lo', 'ilo', elo, or 'elilo'. '10 pounds of gold in my hand in 1 month for my wife's jewelry business' is an example of a postulate or 'ilo'. The intention is to convert the olileanya (vision) into 'e jim n'aka' (certainty, reality, assurance). The vision(s) then creates the 'desire' in the heart. The Heart desire (ife obi m' chọ) then activates the thoughts (Uche) that leads to the actions that yield the gold.

| Chiedo | ⇨ | Vision | ⇨ | Heart | ⇨ | Desire | ⇨ | Action | ⇨ | Purification | ⇨ | Gold |

The word for gold 'edo' contains the verb 'do' which is used in the word udo (peace) , sorry (ndo) and keep (dobe) suggesting it refers to 'chilling' or 'calming' or 'keeping' something. In addition, the verb 'do' is also used in describing someone who looks well and relaxed (arụ i do, onye arụ do). A person who looks well is well kept.

The ability to turn something to gold is a competence that results in well being.

Cause and cause prolongation

Royal meditation makes you the originator and cause over the issues of your life. It makes you wake up and realize that you are projecting your life from the inside out. It gets you to the point where you realize that you are the one doing it. This is what the ancients call Chineme (The Chi is the doer). You are not reacting to crisis every day, but you are creating your own life and causing crisis on earth for the enemies of peace. Then you begin to realize that what your eyes see is not intended to control you. Many live their lives from the outside then in. They are easily controlled by a woman wearing lingerie. The only woman with lingerie that can affect a King is the wife. When a person gets to this level when they can make the gold and not have the gold in Fort Knox control them they understand why the eye is called 'anya.'

Eye (Anya)
'Anya' has two sections 'a' a negative prefix and nya (it), suggesting that the eye is 'not it.'

A royal life is not created by what a person sees but by what they feel inside in the Chi, their personal energy which they reproduce in the physical universe. A person who manifests gold is manifesting the peaceful and golden spirit of Gold and not a shiny metal. There are many worthless metals and objects that outshine gold.

 Meditation gives you access to this golden Chi that creates a loving, joyful and peaceful universe that will obviously need maintenance. If you do not maintain the gold factory, it will shut down. The word for 'cause' is known as 'ifi.' It is the cause, thrust, direction or pulse of a person in the physical universe. Every now and then, people do things because of you. For example, someone can become friends with someone they consider your enemy. It's your ifi (cause) that they are trying to blunt. Prolonging the cause is known as ifite (cause prolongation).

In Igbo land, towns have a sub-town called ifite (cause prolonger) that extends the activities of the village.

Ifite (Cause prolongation) is related to another concept known as 'Otolo.' Otolo contains the words 'oto' (growth) and 'lo' (postulate) and suggests 'growth of a postulate.' The postulate '10 pounds of gold in my hand in 1 month for my wife's jewelry business', needs to be grown to '50 pounds of gold in my hand in one month for the town's jewelry business.' Growth of this postulate is known as 'Otolo' and is related to Ifite (cause prolongation).

> Meditation is your personal ifite (cause prolongation) and Otolo (growth of postulate).

Postulates or Directives

The most exceptional property of the Chi is postulation or direction. This ability of the Chi to postulate or direct is recorded in the phrase Ilochi (postulate of the Chi).

You may have learnt that the Chi is energy (Chidume) or that the Chi is power (Chibụike) but now you know that an exceptional property of the Chi is the ability to postulate or direct. Wealth is a postulate and is known as 'Akụbụilo.' "50 pounds of gold in my hand in 1 month for my jewelry business" is an example of how you make money with postulates or directives.

> **ELOKA-POSTULATION IS GREATER**
>
> Kedụ ife ilo? (What do you postulate?) is greater than Kedụ ife iche (What do you think?).

So I invite you to make your postulate or directives today. The ability of your postulate to turn to reality depends on the condition of your internal energy known as the Chi. This is because postulates come from the Chi. To give you a demonstration, I am postulating that this book will sell 10 million copies in 19 years. Postulation is the greatest and is captured in the phrase known as Eloka (postulation is greater). This is because, a person who gives you the postulate that you will be Royalty is greater than the person who brought you home gave you food or who provided you with accommodation when you were homeless.

Anything you want in your life is available to you through your ability to postulate. Your ability to postulate and have your postulates work depends on the condition of your Chi which depends on the level of investment you have made on the subject of the Chi. The Chi is a physical and non-physical subject but the Chi is designed to work in the physical world of the planet earth. It is designed to make the life of man healthier and happier. The Chi inside you is for your health and happiness.

Examples of postulates or directives

1. I will lose 5 pounds (body weight) this month.
2. I will start taking 30 minutes of brisk walking every other day.
3. I will dance for 10 minutes before taking a shower every day.
4. I will meditate for 20 minutes daily.
5. I will join a social group such as Rotary International before summer.

6. I will double my income in 6 months.
7. I will buy a big house in one year.
8. I will take out a $2 million life insurance before Christmas.
9. I will build my mother a 10 bedroom house so that she will not be lonely anymore by next year.
10. I will stop calling the people I believe are my bad friends, immediately.

Mastering postulates or directives is a special topic. A master of his postulates or directives is known as an Ezeilo (King of Postulates or Directives). The ability of a person to make a postulate that really works obviously depends on their knowledge, experience and mental state. A student who is unemployed and makes the postulate; 'I will make $10 million dollars in one hour' may just be a joker.

Ordinarily, a postulate should not require energy expenditure. It is smooth and happens naturally if a person is highly developed. The postulate; 'My wife will be ok with it' or 'My wife will call once she gets home' does not need enforcing with energy. However, the postulate; "Saddam Hussein and his sons must leave Iraq in 72 hours" may need enforcement by bombs and Marines. A good doctor may give the postulate that 'your weight will be normal in 6 months' without needing to give you drugs with potential life threatening side-effects.

These are some tips for trouble shooting your postulates or directives.

1. Have hope and Faith (See Chapter 2)
2. Consider it done and stop worrying
3. Recalibrate your postulate if you find out it is unreasonable.

4. Take action. E.g. buy yourself a pair of sneakers and map out your walking routes
5. Be determined.
6. Increase your integrity so you are more believable.
7. Enlist allies who share the same goal(s)

Conclusion

This book is an artistic assembly of elements of Igbo culture and meditation. This technique allows you to merge energy (Izu Ike) so you can have surplus energy to achieve your life objectives.

Royal Chi Meditation	
Earthing	Reconciling a person with the earth. Feeling the earth with the feet. Applying the hip to the earth. Being together and speaking together with the earth.
Silence	Applying silence to the world and the troubled Chi (energy) in other to receive from the Earth Energy.
Earth Breathing	Conscious breathing. If possible take abdominal breaths that engage the diaphragm at about 5 breaths per minute.
Hope and Faith	This includes the use of crystals or stones.
Physical activity	A way to increase physical fitness. Walks, squats, stretching, etc.
Postulation	Creating a 'golden' life of your choice from the Chi to the outside world by the use of directives of postulates.

This work is based on the Anambra dialect of the Igbo language.
Ana(Earth) is also known as Ala, Ani, Ali, e.t.c

The future of mankind

My hope is that we begin to create communities and community
leadership based on meditation and the ability to show mercy to
the poor and weak. These communities should not exceed a few
thousand people. They will have a security force of a few dozen
men. No guns are allowed and security will not be armed with
guns. Leadership will be based on ability to demonstrate peace,
love, joy, kindness and philanthropy. These small communities
would be semi-autonomous. They do not necessarily answer to a
President but will pay the necessary taxes for their upkeep. These
communities should be planted simultaneously around the world
and allowed to replace existing social structures. In the end, we
will eliminate guns, armies and war crafts and other weapons of
mass destruction.

The End

Royal meditation will return.

Looking forward to declaring you Royalty

Bonus Material

Evolution of the Chi

Scientists estimate that the Earth is about 4.6 Billion years old and that humans are relatively new arrivals on the surface of this planet.

The first apes with the ability to walk (bipedalism) are thought to have appeared in Africa about 3 million years ago. A combination of internal and environment factors led to evolutionary changes in these early hominids that led to more advanced beings with better abilities that included the design and use of tools, the ability to conquer tough terrain, hunt down large prey, and the development of a compassionate society.

Over the years, internal advancements in ability was expressed through more sophisticated language that developed into more organized communities that were better able to survive environment challenges. These internal advancements led to more capabilities in the environment that can be expressed in the ability to conquer the physical environment that is observable in hill or mountain climbing, swimming, canoeing and other forms of transportation and movement.

Changes in the Chi are thought to have led to changes in human ability. Older authors such as Mbonu Ojike and Chinua Achebe described the Chi as a 'personal god.' According to the ancient Igbo, the Chi is energy and is captured in the phrase 'Chidume.' The Chi is also the power or energy behind a person and is captured in the phrase (Chibuike). Chijindu means that the Chi holds life.

The life of a person is directed from the internal Chi to the outside world and physical universe. All human experiences occur in the Chi. If you lost a parent and you go to a cemetery where your loved one is buried to grieve, the experience is only possible in the Chi. Without the Chi, you will have no lost parent to mourn and no idea what it means to loose or bury a parent. The feelings and the experiences that draw a person to the grave-side to mourn are in the Chi. The feelings and emotions that compel a person to neglect his parents or care for a child are also in the Chi. The observable neglect or care is a translation of the energy directed from the Chi.

Developments in human life that has occurred over thousands of years are thought to have occurred simultaneously in the Chi. Without changes in the Chi of Americans, slavery would not have ended and people would still be lynched and flogged in the streets.

Cycles in life

Simply put, Igbo culture revolves around the things that happen on earth. These activities come in different cycles. In ancient times, it started with morning meditation and then the children may have to clean their teeth before going to fetch water in the stream, eat breakfast, then start playing etc. This cycle repeats itself every day. An adult may have to start with meditation, cleaning oneself up, eating breakfast and then setting out to the farm or for a hunt (if a hunter). This cycle repeats itself every day. In the modern world, the cycle is more or less the same. There is also the cycle of birth, marriage and death. These are all the cycles that occur in the earth (Earth happenings, Omenana) and meditation prepares you to participate in these cycles in your best mental form.

There is also a cycle of day and night. This cycle has Chi names; Chi ifo (day) and Chi iji (night, darkness). The verb 'fo' is to unfold, suggesting that day is the unfolding of the Chi, while night is the darkening of the Chi. It is not surprising that the Chi, the personal energy is associated with the sky because day and night affects a person's energy and destiny. Blind people, for instance, are known to be resistant to certain types of Cancer.

The word Chi is also the word for 'end', so the Sky is a type of back end. It contains the celestial objects, the sun, moon, and the stars which are known to be relevant to life on earth. Early suspicion as to the significance of these celestial objects in human destiny may have led to the development of astrology and similar practices.

Important Notice: The Igbo language is verb based. Actions were translated into verbs that are identified by their sound. There are some verbs that sound phonologically slightly different from each other. These verbs represent similar actions. The difference could be because the activities are performed in different environments, e.g. in the physical or non-physical planes. It can also be due to the presence of prefixes or suffixes that modify the sound of the verb. For example, the name Chịka is from 'Chi' and 'ka.' The 'ị' in Chika sounds slightly phonologically different from the 'i' in Chi, but both convey the same message. Igbo is also polysemic-one word can have different meanings. For example, anụ could refer to animal, beast, fresh meat, cooked meat, or even a fool.

The Earth

The earth is billions of years old and is considered an authority in Igbo. The earth can be considered in religious circles as a deity. That means the earth has the capacity to punish or bless. 'Anagọlu' is a word that has the root word for bless 'gọ' which suggests 'blessed by the Earth.' In fact, a common word for Igbo culture is 'Omenana' which suggests 'Happening on the Earth' or 'Earth Happenings.' This suggests that Igbo life revolves around the Earth and that a favorable relationship with the earth is a necessity for a good pleasant life.

The Chi is the source of experiences

The Igbo people correctly made a very important statement that is often neglected; 'things come from the Chi/Ife si na Chi.' This statement suggest that our experiences in life actually come from within, the Chi.

One of the challenges of the modern human is to develop the capacity to experience their choice. For example, one may prefer to listen to the sound of nature at night rather than living next to the highway or railway and being continuously disturbed by noisy traffic. Meditation gives one access to higher consciousness and the Chi, so that we can begin an endless journey to manifest our choosing, that is being cause, rather than being the effect of the universe.

Man is unique because of our ability to work together on common goals. For example, the US Defense force has manpower of hundreds of thousands of individuals. Unlike, the wildebeest in the Serengeti that also number hundreds of thousands; humans are able to deploy tools such as Tanks and Aircraft that have enormous impact on geography and terrain. The ability of the US Defense forces to mount an effective response depends on effective communication between hundreds and thousands of Chi communicating and coordinating their experiences and actions.

Speaking with the earth.

'I tu kwu ana' (sitting on the earth) contains the verbs I (positive prefix), tu (oneness), kwu (speak) and Ana (earth). The verb 'tu' is used in the word for One (Otu), Group (Otu) and Nail (Ntu) and suggests 'oneness' or 'unity.' The Lotus position is a way to achieve 'oneness' or 'unity' with the earth which is an authority with the ability to bless. This association with the earth is important especially considering that some evolutionary psychologists believe that higher consciousness developed in lower animals as non-physical, energy saving mechanism that helps in navigating the earth.

Boy sitting on the earth (I tu kwu ana). Courtesy of Ojike, 1946.

The man sitting on a chair is an 'Amana' which is a high profile community position comparable to a Legislator. 'I ma ana' (to know the Earth) is the art of knowing your town which every Legislator should be competent in for proper representation of their constituents. An 'Amana' obviously knows his way around the community or has 'Earth Knowledge.' Ojike is standing to the far right.

Etymologically speaking, 'I tu kwu ana' (sitting on the earth) is a way to speak in unity with the earth. To give you a clearer picture of this position, I would like to introduce you to the word for waist which is 'ukwu.' Ukwu contains the verb 'kwu' which is 'speak.' The waist is used in non-verbal 'speaking' or communication and I will elaborate further under the section hope. The waist is the anatomical structure used to contact and communicate with the earth. It has relevance in sitting and lying on the earth while meditating. 'Nọ du ana' is another phrase for 'sitting on the earth and is derived from nọ (togetherness, du (being) and ana (earth). 'Nọ du ana' is 'be together with the earth.'

Etymological considerations of Silence

Silence is known simply as 'igba nkiti' (apply silence) or as 'igba ụwa nkiti' (apply silence to the world around) or 'Igba Chi nkiti (apply silence to the Chi). Chi, which we now know as the 'personal energy' is also the word for 'end.' This is because the Chi is the 'end' from which we emerge and our lives are created. It is like the back end of the Theatre from which the actors emerge or the back end of a computer or computer software. The word 'end' does not suggest inferiority but rather is communicating 'source.'

The intent of meditation is to connect an individual to loving and peaceful universal energy from which we are made from. We do this by connecting to the universal energy in the earth through the waist. We also need to silence our personal energy (the Chi), during meditation, because it is affected by the negative energy accumulated by encountering other humans and other life challenges.

In this period of silence, we are communicating with the peaceful soul, the universal energy, the earth energy which is a loving peaceful energy. This energy does not necessarily speak a human language as in vocal words but humans can translate this communication into human words and action. Typically, the communication is about positive emotions or energy such as love, peace and joy. This energy of peace, love and joy can be translated into thoughts, words and action of peace, love and joy. A peaceful Chi (personal energy) is known as 'Udochi.' Evidence of meditation, is seen in the community as acts of kindness and philanthropy.

Expressing the loving energy of the earth is embodied in the principle of Anagekwu (the earth will speak) which allows an individual to contact and communicate peaceful and loving information from the earth. Anakwu (Earth speak) and Anakwue (Earth speaking) are variants of this principle.

Meditation while lying down

To better understand the pattern of Igbo meditation, I would like to introduce you to the word for 'lie down' known as 'Di nọ Ana.' 'Di nọ ana' literally means 'lie together with the Earth', that is if you would like to make a simple translation. The verb 'nọ' refers to togetherness and is used in the word for home 'Unọ' and 'sticking together.' The verb 'Di' is used in a wide range of words in the Igbo language.

Di	Use
Di	Husband
Di nọ ana	Lie down on earth
Di Azụ	Fisher man or Di Fish
Di nta	Hunter or Di Hunting

Idi	Forgiveness
Di	**Rightness, Wellness, Well being, Well, Mastery**

Although, some have defined 'Di' as 'Master', I strongly believe that Di refers to rightness, wellness, and proficiency. This is because its close variant, Di, refers to well being and is used in Dili (Be well, Wellness).

This makes 'Di nọ ana' or 'lie down'; 'be well together with the earth'. This is because the Earth is a source of Healing and wellness. This is not unique in Igbo, the Earth is also recognized for its healing qualities in Yoga, Tai Chi and similar culturally based healing and relaxation techniques.

So, one of the first steps in Igbo meditation is to begin to reconcile one with the earth by sitting and/or lying down on the earth. Even in the Christian Bible, the earth is also associated with healing; '....He makes me lie down in green pastures, He leads me beside the still waters, He restores my soul (Psalm, 23).' I recommend lying down on the earth proper, as in lying on the grass over a mat. If you want to meditate inside the house, I recommend going down stairs to lie on a portion that has direct connection to the basement of the house that is directly connected to the earth. At the same time, I do not see anything wrong with meditating upstairs.

So again, the first step is to be together with the earth.

Hips and communication

The word for buttocks or butts is known as 'Ike' and is phonetically and phonologically very similar to Ike (power). It is not unreasonable to assume that women with bigger 'buttocks' were able to contact and communicate this peaceful and joyful information better and may have helped drive the evolution of sizeable buttocks in humans. Today, buttock size is a desirable quality of beauty in all cultures. Women with these larger buttocks provided they are not too large, are obviously better able to attract mates and is probably a powerful advantage. This may be the origin of the phrase 'bottom power.'

The female waist is part of a cycle that keeps hope alive in the community. It is a communication tool between a woman and the earth, between woman and men in the desire for love, and a communication tool between a woman and the community, all the time expressing the hope for love, peace and joy.

While dancing, if possible, the eyes should be closed so that one can concentrate in internal sensations. This is a way to be with the Chi and allow the Chi to be in control.

Okwụlụ (Okra) contains the verb 'kwụlụ' which is 'stand.' Okra is believed by Physicians to contain polysaccharides that are helpful in penile erections, hence the name 'plant Viagra.'
Make your own plant Viagra by placing sliced okra in filtered water. Drink the slimy juice, as often as necessary.

Postulates

The verb 'lo' is the root word for postulate and is preserved in the word Chibụilo (Chi is postulate), Elochukwu (postulate of God), Ezeilo (King of postulate) , Ilochi (postulate of the Chi), Chilo (Chi postulate), ilo (strong postulate), elo (postulate), and elilo (postulating).

Ilo (Postulate or directive) is phonologically very similar to Ilo

---

(enmity) and is a common source of confusion among modern Igbos. These words share a similar verb because it is our postulates that create enmity for us. A person who was never born or who never made any postulates will not have any 'enemies.' But once, you make the postulate; 'I will be President in 2050', snap, your enemies will show up behind you or in front of you. The confusion between ilo(postulate) and ilo(enmity) makes some believe that Chibụilo means 'the Chi is enmity 'or that Akụbụilo is 'wealth is enmity.' The latter assumption may prevent some individuals from pursuing wealth in the erroneous belief that having money will get them killed.

Acknowledgements.

I would like to acknowledge Ezeokoli and Sarah Ezenwosu (Grandparents), Lawrence and Cecilia Okeke (Grandparents) , Mike and Bridget Nwosu (Parents), Dr.John and Uche Nwosu (Uncle & Aunt), Richard Brown, MD, (Breath Body Mind), Pat Gerbarg, MD, (Breath Body Mind), Oscar Mokeme, MA (elements of Royal Dance), Justice Obi, MD, RPh(back breathing), Ambassador Marius Offor, Barrack Obama, Nelson Mandela, Martin Luther King Jr., Gandhi, Nick Muoneke, PhD, and many others too numerous to mention that stood for the dignity of man.

DISCLAIMER: The use of 'names' in this work is for educational purposes only. These names are not intended to refer to any individual living or dead, except when clearly referring to a particular individual.

BIBLIOGRAPHY

1. Achebe, Chinua. Things Fall Apart. Anchor Books -- Doubleday, NYC (January 1, 1994)
2. Achebe, Chinua. No Longer at Ease. Heinemann, 1960.
3. Achebe, Chinua. Arrow of God. Heinemann, 1964.
4. Achebe, Chinua. There was a country: a personal history of Biafra. © 2013 Penguin.
5. Aguwa, Jude C. U. (1995). The Agwu deity in Igbo religion. Fourth Dimension Publishing Co., Ltd. ISBN 978-156-399-0.
6. Ambrose, Stanley H. (March 2, 2001). "Paleolithic Technology and Human Evolution". Science (Washington, D.C.: American Association for the Advancement of Science) 291 (5509): 1748–1753.
7. Anunobi, Chikodili. Nri Warriors of Peace. Zenith Press; 1 edition (February 28, 2006).
8. Baars, Bernard J. A Cognitive Theory of Consciousness. 1993. Cambridge University Press.

9. Basden, George Thomas (1921). Among the Ibos of Nigeria. Nonsuch Publishing
10. Botha, R. and C. Knight (eds) 2009. The Cradle of Language. Oxford: Oxford University Press.
11. Brown, RP and Gerbarg, P. The Healing Power of the breath. 2012 Shambhala publications.
12. Brown RP, Gerbarg PL, Muench F Breathing practices for treatment of psychiatric and stress-related medical conditions.Psychiatr Clin North Am. 2013

13. Cant, John Hypothesis for the Evolution of Human Breasts and Buttocks *The American Naturalist* Vol. 117, No. 2 (Feb., 1981), pp. 199-204.

14. Date Sex @ University of Pennsylvania Museum of Archaeology and Anthropology. http://www.penn.museum/

15. Davidson, R and Begley S. The emotional life of your brain: How its unique patterns affect the way you think , feel and live-and how you can change them. © 2012 Plume.

16. Deacon, Terrence W. (1997) The Symbolic Species: The Co-evolution of Language and the Brain. W.W. Norton & Co

17. Diamond, Jared *(1999).* Guns, Germs, and Steel: The Fates of Human Societies. *New York:* W. W. Norton & Company. ISBN 0-393-31755-2. LCCN 2005284124. OCLC 35792200

18. Dolgoff-Kasper, Baldwin A, Johnson S, Edling N, Sethi GK. Effect of laughter on mood and heart rate variability in patients awaiting organ transplantation: a pilot study. Altern Ther Health Med. 2012 Jul-Aug; 18 (4): 53-8.

19. Dollar, Creflo. Experiencing God's Love. A guide for new believers. Creflo Dollar Ministries ISBN 1-59089-806-0.

20. Eccles, J. C. (1992). "Evolution of consciousness". Proceedings of the National Academy of Sciences of the United States of America 89 (16): 7320–4. *doi*:10.1073/pnas.89.16.7320. *JSTOR* 2360081. *PMC* 49701. *PMID* 1502142.

21. Ejizu, Christopher. Ofo; Igbo ritual and symbol. Fourth Dimension Publishing Co. (March 11, 2002).

22. Feychting M, Osterlund B, Ahlbom A. Reduced cancer incidence among the blind. Epidemiology. 1998 Sep;9(5):490-4.

23. Fitch. W. Tecumseh The Evolution of Language. Cambridge University Press pp. 65–66. (2010).

24. Frantzis, Bruce Kumar . The Chi Revolution: Harnessing the Healing Power of Your Life Force. Blue Snake Books. ISBN 1-58394-193-2.
25. Freeman and Herron. Evolutionary Analysis. 2007. Pearson Education, NJ.
26. Frey Bruno S Happy People Live Longer, , Science 4 February 2011: 542-543.
27. Gallup. State of the American Workplace Report 2013.
28. Gaulin and McBurney 2003 p. 101-121.
29. Gerber M[1], Brand S, Elliot C, Holsboer-Trachsler E, Pühse U Aerobic Exercise, Ball Sports, Dancing, and weight lifting as moderators of the relationship between stress and depressive symptoms: an exploratory cross-sectional study with Swiss University Students. Percept Mot Skills. 2014 Dec;119(3):679-697.
30. Holt, Stephen. Combat Syndrom X, Y, Z. Wellness publishing (2002).
31. Holt, Stephen. A certification program for dietary supplement councilors. Holt Institute of Medicine press © 2008. www.hiom.org
32. Holt, Stephen. The definitive guide to colon hydrotherapy: Principles and Practice of Colonic Irrigation. © 2013 Holt Institute of Medicine.
33. Holt, Stephen. Sleep naturally. © 2003 Wellness publishing.
34. Holt, Stephen. Sex the natural way.(c) 2011 Holt Institute of Medicine.
35. http://en.wikipedia.org/wiki/Shalom
36. Ilogu, Edmund (1974). Christianity and Ibo culture. Brill. ISBN 90-04-04021-8
37. Isichei, Elizabeth Allo (1997). A History of African Societies to 1870. Cambridge University Press. p. 247. ISBN 0-521-45599-5.
38. Johanson, Donald.

Origins of Modern Humans: Multiregional or Out of Africa?http://www.actionbioscience.org/evolution/johanson.html

39. Koike MK, Cardoso R. Meditation can produce beneficial effects to prevent cardiovascular disease. Horm Mol Biol Clin Investig. 2014 Jun;18(3):137-43. doi: 10.1515/hmbci-2013-0056.

40. Kong M, Shin SH, Lee E, Yun EK. The effect of laughter therapy on radiation dermatitis in patients with breast cancer: a single-blind prospective pilot study. Onco Targets Ther. 2014 Nov 4;7:2053-9. doi: 10.2147/OTT.S72973. eCollection 2014.

41. Lindsay, David (2000). *House of invention : the secret life of everyday products*. New York, N.Y.: Lyons Press. p. 20-21

42. *Mcbrearty, Sally; Brooks, Alison S. (November 2000).* "The revolution that wasn't: a new interpretation of the origin of modern human behavior". Journal of Human Evolution *(Amsterdam, the Netherlands:* Elsevier*) 39 (5): 453–563.*

43. *McHenry, Henry M. (2009). "Human Evolution". In* Ruse, Michael; Travis, Joseph. *Evolution: The First Four Billion Years. Foreword by* Edward O. Wilson. *Cambridge, MA:* Belknap Press of Harvard University Press. ISBN 978-0-674-03175-3. LCCN 2008030270. OCLC 225874308.

44. *Miller, Matt.* Bounce: Rap Music and Local Identity in New Orleans. Boston: Univ of Massachusetts Press, 2012.

45. Murrock CJ[1], Graor CH. Effects of dance on depression, physical function, and disability in underserved adults. J Aging Phys Act. 2014 Jul;22(3):380-5. doi: 10.1123/japa.2013-0003. Epub 2013 Aug 12.

46. Nichols, S.; Grantham, T. (2000). "Adaptive Complexity and Phenomenal Consciousness". Philosophy of Science *67 (4): 648–70.* doi:10.1086/392859. JSTOR 188711.

47. Nwafor, Chukwukadibia. Leopards of the Magical dawn © 2014 lulu.com

48. Nwosu, Uzoma. Igbo voices; hidden wisdom from an ancient language. © 2013

49. Nwosu, Uzoma. Chi, and healing words from an ancient language. © 2013

50. Nwosu, Uzoma. The Chiology way to happiness. © 2014.

51. Ogomaka, P.M.C, (in press), 'Number Systems including some Indigenous Number Systems'. Teaching Modules for Secondary School Teachers of General Mathematics, Abuja: NMC

52. Ogomaka, P.M.C. & Akukwe, A.C., 1998, 'School and Work place Mathematics in Imo State: Some implications', Nigerian Journal of Curriculum and Instruction, Vol. 7, No 1:13-18

53. Ohuche, R.O, Ezeilo, J.O.C; Eke, B. I, et al., 1986, Everyday Mathematics for the Junior Secondary School, Book 1, Enugu: Fourth Dimension Publishers.

54. Ojike, Mbonu, My Africa, 1946.

55. Olaudah Equiano, The Interesting Narrative of the Life of Olaudah Equiano, or Gustavus Vassa, the African. Simon & Brown publishers.

56. Onwuejeogwu, M. Angulu (1981). An Igbo civilization: Nri kingdom & hegemony. Ethnographica. ISBN 978-123-105-X.

57. Pamela J. W. Gore (1996-01-22). "Phases of the Moon". Georgia Perimeter College. http://facstaff.gpc.edu/~pgore/astronomy/astr101/moon phas.htm

58. Patrick Mathias Chukwuaku Ogomaka. Traditional Igbo Numbering System: A Reconstruction. Africa Development, Vol. XXX, No.3, 2005, pp. 35–47 © Council

for the Development of Social Science Research in Africa, 2005 (ISSN 0850-3907).

59. Peters, Frederic "Consciousness as Recursive, Spatiotemporal Self-Location". http://precedings.nature.com/documents/2444/version/1

60. Revolutionary War Exhibit Text - November 2002

61. Salerno, John P. The Salerno Solution. © 2013 Take Charge books.

62. Schwager, E. "From Petroleum Jelly to Riches". *Drug News & Perspectives* **11** (2): p. 127.

63. Singleton, Alena J. (2008). "Cultural History of the Buttocks". In Pitts-Taylor, Victoria. Cultural Encyclopedia of the Body. ABC-CLIO/Greenwood. ISBN 978-0-313-34145-8

64. Streeter CC, Gerbarg PL, Saper MD, Ciraulo DA, and Brown RP. Effects of yoga on the autonomic nervous system, gamma-aminobutyric-acid, and allostasis in epilepsy, depression, and Post-traumatic Stress Disorder. Medical Hypotheses. 2012. May;78(5):571-9.

65. Stringer, Chris B. (1994) [First published 1992]. "Evolution of Early Humans". In Jones, Steve; *Martin, Robert D.;* Pilbeam, David. The Cambridge Encyclopedia of Human Evolution.

66. Stringer C. Human evolution: Out of Ethiopia. Nature. 2003 Jun 12;423(6941):692-3, 695.

67. Sylvester Okwunodu Ogbechie,: Ben Enwonwu: the making of an African modernist. University Rochester Press, 2008.

68. The Holy Bible.

69. Tolle, Eckhart. The Power of Now: A Guide to Spiritual Enlighenment. New world library, 2004

70. Tolle, Eckhart. A New Earth. Awakening to your Life's purpose. Penguin, 2008.Twerking, https://en.wikipedia.org/wiki/Twerking

71. Uchendu, Victor C. The Igbo of Southeast Nigeria. Van Nostrand Reinhold Company, 1965.

72. Udeani, Chibueze C. (2007). Inculturation as dialogue: Igbo culture and the message of Christ. Rodopi. p. 28—29. ISBN 90-420-2229-9.

73. Uzukwu, E. Elochukwu (1997). Worship as body language: introduction to Christian worship : an African orientation. Liturgical Press. ISBN 0-8146-6151-3.

74. Woodbury-Fariña MA, Antongiorgi JL Humor. Psychiatr Clin North Am. 2014 Dec;37(4):561-578. doi: 10.1016/j.psc.2014.08.006. Epub 2014 Nov 25.

75. Yeung A, Kiat H, Denniss AR, Cheema BS, Bensoussan A, Machliss B, Colagiuri B, Chang D Randomised controlled trial of a 12 week yoga intervention on negative affective states, cardiovascular and cognitive function in post-cardiac rehabilitation patients. BMC Complement Altern Med. 2014 Oct 24;14:411. doi: 10.1186/1472-6882-14-411.

76. Zhang X, Ni X, Chen P. Study about the effects of different fitness sports on cognitive function and emotion of the aged. Cell Biochem Biophys. 2014 Dec;70(3):1591-6. doi: 10.1007/s12013-014-0100-8.

.

Books by the Author.

1. Uzoma Nwosu, MD. Igbo voices; hidden wisdom from an ancient language. ©2013
2. Uzoma Nwosu, MD. Chi, and healing words from an ancient language © 2013
3. Stephen Holt MD, Uzoma Nwosu, MD, Clifford Carroll. The Topical Pain Relief Revolution: Principles and Practice of Compounding Pharmacy. © 2013 Holt Institute of Medicine.
4. Uzoma Nwosu, MD. The Chiology way to happiness © 2014.
5. Uzoma Nwosu, MD Igbo voices: advancing the Chi. © 2015

About the Author

Dr. Uzoma Nwosu was born in Enugu, the former capital of Eastern Nigeria. He grew up with his Igbo family and was surrounded by grandparents, Uncles, Aunts and other relatives that were highly exposed to Igbo custom known as Omenana. Following graduation from college of Medicine, University of Nigeria, he worked as a Medical Officer at the General Hospital Onitsha as well as the Brigade of Guards Medical Center in Abuja.

In South Africa, he started as a Medical Officer at the South Rand Hospital, subsequently rising to a Principal Medical Officer at the Department of Medico-Legal Services, Johannesburg.

Dr. Nwosu held research positions in the Pharmaceutical industry in South Africa. He worked in the Clinical Research department in Abbott Laboratories and was a Medical Advisor at Pharmacia/Pfizer.

In the United States, he worked as a Research Fellow, at the NYU Hospital for Joint Diseases.

Dr. Nwosu has Holistic and Integrative Medicine experience having worked with Dr. Stephen Holt at Natural Clinician and Dr. Richard Brown at Breath Body Mind.

Chiology was born out of all his combined experiences and a need to deliver a Holistic healing technique that is based on African culture, specifically Omenana (Earth Happenings, Earth Culture).

Dr. Nwosu is from a long line of the high ranking Ozo Priests and also has royal blood from his Igbo ancestry.

www.chiology.org

Index

www.ingramcontent.com/pod-product-compliance
Lightning Source LLC
Chambersburg PA
CBHW072210090426
42740CB00012B/2461